BIG BUCKS WITH MOBILE HOMES

CAPITALIZE ON THIS HIDDEN NICHE OF REAL ESTATE INVESTING FOR BIG PROFITS AND CASH FLOW

ADAM VOEGTLI

Contents

1

INTRODUCTION

The world of real estate investing is vast, and there are many different types of properties to choose from. However, few options can offer the same combination of low entry costs, strong cash flow, and steady demand as mobile homes. Investing in mobile homes is a unique and often overlooked investment strategy that can be highly lucrative for those who take the time to understand the market and its nuances.

If you're interested in investing in real estate but don't have the capital to purchase a traditional home, mobile homes may be an excellent option for you. The lower cost of entry is a major advantage of mobile home investing, as the price of a mobile home is typically a fraction of the cost of a traditional home. This means that even novice investors can get started in mobile home investing without a significant financial commitment.

Another advantage of mobile home investing is the potential for high returns. With lower entry costs, mobile home investors can achieve a higher cash-on-cash return compared to traditional real estate investments. In some cases, mobile home investors can generate returns of 20% or more per year, making it a highly attractive investment strategy.

In addition to the low entry costs and high returns, mobile homes are in high demand, especially in areas where affordable housing is limited. This means that there is a steady demand for mobile homes, which translates to a lower vacancy rate and higher potential for cash flow. Mobile homes are often rented by people who are just starting out, young couples, or retirees, making them a popular choice for a wide range of tenants.

Despite the many advantages of mobile home investing, there are also some perceived risks and challenges that come with this type of investment. For example, many investors are concerned about the potential for damage to the mobile home during transportation, as well as the risk of tenants not paying rent or causing damage to the property. However, these risks can be mitigated with proper due diligence and management.

This book aims to provide a comprehensive guide to investing in mobile homes, covering everything from the types of mobile home investments available to how to finance your investments and manage your properties. We'll also discuss the legal considerations involved in mobile home investing, as well as the risks and rewards of this type of investment.

If you're new to real estate investing or looking for a way to diversify your portfolio, investing in mobile homes may be the perfect strategy for you. In this book, we'll provide you with the knowledge and tools you need to succeed in this unique and potentially lucrative market. So let's get started and explore the world of mobile home investing together!

Part of what makes investing in mobile homes such an attractive option is the opportunity to generate strong cash flow. Because mobile homes are typically rented out, investors can earn regular rental income that can exceed their expenses, which can include the cost of the property itself, insurance, taxes, and other maintenance costs. With the potential for high cash-on-cash returns, mobile homes can be a great option for investors looking to generate passive income.

Mobile homes also offer investors the opportunity to diversify their real estate portfolio. Investing in mobile homes can provide a hedge against traditional real estate investments that are typically more expensive and require a larger upfront investment. By diversifying your real estate investments, you can reduce your exposure to market fluctuations and other economic risks.

This book is designed to be a comprehensive guide for investors interested in mobile home investing, regardless of their experience level. Whether you're new to real estate investing or a seasoned investor, this book will provide you with the information and tools you need to succeed in this unique market.

In the following chapters, we'll dive into the specifics of investing in mobile homes, including the different types of mobile home investments, how to find and evaluate properties, how to finance your investments, and how to manage your properties. We'll also discuss the legal considerations involved in mobile home investing and the risks and rewards of this type of investment.

By the end of this book, you'll have a thorough understanding of the mobile home market, as well as the tools and resources you need to succeed as a mobile home investor. So let's get started and discover the world of mobile home investing together!

Before we dive into the specifics of mobile home investing, it's important to address some common misconceptions about mobile homes. While some people may view mobile homes as inferior or low-quality, the reality is that they have come a long way in terms of design and construction. Modern mobile homes are often built to the same quality standards as traditional homes, and many even include high-end amenities like granite countertops, stainless steel appliances, and energy-efficient features.

Another misconception about mobile homes is that they are a risky investment. While any investment comes with risks, mobile homes can be a safe and profitable investment when done correctly. With the right due diligence and management, investors can mitigate the risks associated with mobile home investing and enjoy a steady stream of passive income.

In the following chapters, we'll cover everything you need to know to start investing in mobile homes, including how to find and evaluate properties, how to finance your investments, and how to manage your properties. We'll also discuss the legal considerations involved in mobile home investing, such as state and federal regulations, and the different types of mobile home investments, including rental mobile homes, flipping mobile homes, and mobile home parks.

One of the most important aspects of mobile home investing is due diligence. Before you invest in a mobile home, it's essential to conduct a thorough inspection of the property and ensure that it meets your investment criteria. In this book, we'll provide you with a guide to evaluating mobile homes and conducting due diligence, so you can make informed decisions and avoid costly mistakes.

We'll also discuss the various financing options available to mobile home investors, including traditional bank loans, private lenders, and creative financing strategies. Understanding your financing options is critical to ensuring the success of your mobile home investment.

Throughout the book, we'll also provide practical tips and advice from experienced mobile home investors, as well as case studies of successful mobile home investments. By learning from the experiences of others, you can avoid common mistakes and ensure the success of your own mobile home investments.

Investing in mobile homes is a unique and potentially lucrative opportunity for investors of all levels of experience. By reading this book and following the strategies and advice provided, you can take advantage of this exciting and profitable investment option. So let's get started and discover the world of mobile home investing together!

2

WHAT YOU'RE GETTING INTO WITH MOBILE HOMES

When it comes to real estate investing, there are many options to choose from, including traditional homes, apartment buildings, commercial properties, and more. However, mobile homes offer a unique set of advantages that other real estate investments can't match. In this chapter, we'll explore some of the reasons why mobile homes are a great investment option.

A. Low Cost of Entry

One of the most significant advantages of mobile home investing is the low cost of entry. Mobile homes are typically much less expensive than traditional homes, making them an excellent option for novice investors or those with limited capital. In some cases, you can purchase a mobile home for as little as $5,000, while traditional homes can cost upwards of $200,000.

The low cost of entry means that investors can get started with mobile home investing with relatively little capital. This is particularly appealing to novice investors who are just starting in the real estate market and may not have the resources to purchase traditional homes or apartments. Mobile homes offer a low-risk way to start investing in real estate without a significant upfront investment.

The lower cost of entry also means that investors can achieve a higher cash-on-cash return compared to traditional real estate investments. With a lower upfront investment, investors can earn a higher percentage return on their investment, making mobile homes a highly attractive investment strategy.

B. Potential for High Returns

Another advantage of mobile home investing is the potential for high returns. While the returns will vary depending on the type of investment and location, mobile homes can generate strong cash flow and provide excellent returns for investors.

Mobile homes offer a great opportunity for investors to generate passive income through rental income. In some cases, the monthly rent for a mobile home can be equivalent to or even higher than the rent for a traditional home or apartment. For example, a mobile home that is rented out for $500 per month could generate a gross annual rent of $6,000. After accounting for expenses such as property taxes, insurance, and maintenance, an investor could earn a net income of $4,000 or more per year.

With a low upfront investment, investors can achieve a cash-on-cash return of 20% or more, making mobile homes a highly attractive investment option.

C. Steady Demand

Another advantage of mobile home investing is the steady demand for affordable housing. Mobile homes are an attractive option for many renters, especially in areas where affordable housing is limited. They offer a more affordable alternative to traditional homes or apartments, making them a popular choice for young couples, retirees, and others who are just starting out.

The demand for mobile homes is not likely to decrease anytime soon. According to the Manufactured Housing Institute, there are currently around 22 million people living in mobile homes in the United States, and this number is expected to grow in the coming years.

Investors can take advantage of this steady demand by purchasing mobile homes in areas where affordable housing is in high demand. By renting out these homes to renters, investors can earn steady rental income while also contributing to the growing need for affordable housing.

D. Strong Cash Flow

Mobile homes can provide strong cash flow for investors, thanks to the lower costs of ownership and the steady demand for affordable housing. With lower upfront costs and lower operating expenses, mobile homes can generate higher cash flow compared to traditional real estate investments.

For example, a mobile home that is rented out for $500 per month could generate a gross annual rent of $6,000. After accounting for expenses such as property taxes, insurance, and maintenance, an investor could earn a net income of $4,000 or more per year. This can provide a steady stream of passive income for investors, making mobile homes an excellent option for those looking to generate long-term wealth.

E. Flexibility in Location

Another advantage of mobile home investing is the flexibility in location. Because mobile homes can be transported from one location to another, investors have the ability to invest in different markets and take advantage of different economic conditions.

For example, if one market becomes oversaturated or starts to decline, an investor can transport the mobile home to a new location where demand is higher. This flexibility can provide a level of protection against market fluctuations and other economic risks.

The ability to transport mobile homes also offers investors the flexibility to take advantage of emerging markets or underserved areas. If an investor identifies a market where affordable housing is in high demand, they can transport a mobile home to that location and begin generating rental income in a relatively short amount of time.

The flexibility in location also means that investors can spread their risk across different markets. If an investor has several mobile homes in different markets, they can reduce their exposure to market fluctuations in any one particular area. This can help to protect their investments against market risks and other economic uncertainties.

F. Lower Maintenance Costs

Mobile homes are typically smaller and more straightforward in design than traditional homes, which means that maintenance costs can be lower. Additionally, many mobile homes are built with durable and long-lasting materials, which can reduce the need for costly repairs over time.

Lower maintenance costs can translate to higher profits for investors, as they will have fewer expenses to deduct from their rental income. This can also make mobile homes a more attractive option for investors who prefer to be more hands-off when it comes to property management.

G. Investment Diversification

Mobile home investing can also provide an opportunity for investors to diversify their real estate portfolio. By investing in mobile homes in addition to traditional homes, apartment buildings, or commercial properties, investors can spread their risk and reduce their exposure to market fluctuations and other economic risks.

Investing in mobile homes can also provide a hedge against traditional real estate investments that are typically more expensive and require a larger upfront investment. By diversifying your real estate investments, you can reduce your exposure to market fluctuations and other economic risks.

In summary, investing in mobile homes offers a unique set of advantages that make it an attractive investment option for investors of all levels of experience. With their low cost of entry, potential for high returns, steady demand, strong cash flow, flexibility in location, lower maintenance costs, and investment diversification, mobile homes can be a profitable addition to any real estate portfolio. By understanding the benefits of mobile home investing, you can make informed investment decisions and build a profitable portfolio of mobile home investments. Sure, here are a few more points to expand on in the "Why Mobile Homes Are a Great Investment" section:

H. Growing Demand for Affordable Housing

Mobile homes are becoming an increasingly popular option for those seeking affordable housing. As traditional home and rental prices continue to rise, mobile homes offer an attractive alternative for those looking for affordable housing options.

According to the Manufactured Housing Institute, the average price of a new manufactured home in 2020 was $87,200, compared to an average price of $383,900 for a new site-built home. This cost difference makes mobile homes a more accessible option for many Americans who may not be able to afford traditional homes.

Mobile homes are also an appealing option for those looking for a more sustainable and eco-friendly living option. Many new mobile homes are built with energy-efficient materials and appliances, which can help to reduce energy costs and minimize their environmental impact.

Investors can take advantage of this growing demand for affordable housing by investing in mobile homes in areas where housing costs are high. By renting out these homes to renters, investors can earn steady rental income while also contributing to the growing need for affordable housing.

I. Ability to Upgrade and Add Value

Mobile homes offer the ability to upgrade and add value, which can increase their resale value and rental income potential. Investors can make strategic upgrades to mobile homes to increase their overall value, such as adding new appliances, installing energy-efficient features, or adding additional living space.

By upgrading mobile homes, investors can increase their rental income potential, making these properties even more attractive from an investment standpoint. Additionally, these upgrades can help to increase the overall value of the mobile home, making it more attractive to potential buyers if the investor decides to sell the property.

J. Strong Resale Value

Mobile homes can hold their resale value well over time, making them a more stable investment option than some other types of real estate investments. Unlike traditional homes, mobile homes can be manufactured to higher standards, which helps to ensure that they retain their value over time.

Additionally, mobile homes are often located in desirable areas, such as near waterfronts, parks, and other recreational areas. This can help to increase the resale value of the property, as buyers may be willing to pay a premium for these types of locations.

K. Tax Benefits

Investing in mobile homes can also offer tax benefits to investors. Like traditional real estate investments, mobile homes can be depreciated over time, which can provide a significant tax deduction for investors.

Additionally, investors can deduct expenses related to owning and operating the mobile home, such as property taxes, insurance, and maintenance costs. These deductions can help to reduce the overall tax liability for the investor, making mobile homes an even more attractive investment option.

In summary, investing in mobile homes offers a unique set of advantages that make it an attractive investment option for investors of all levels of experience. With their low cost of entry, potential for high returns, steady demand, strong cash flow, flexibility in location, lower maintenance costs, investment diversification, growing demand for affordable housing, ability to upgrade and add value, strong resale value, and tax benefits, mobile homes can be a profitable addition to any real estate portfolio. By understanding the benefits of mobile home investing, you can make informed investment decisions and build a profitable portfolio of mobile home investments.

3

WHAT YOU'RE LOOKING FOR WHEN IT COMES TO MOBILE HOMES

Mobile home investing offers a variety of different investment options for investors. In this chapter, we'll explore several different types of mobile home investments, including rental mobile homes, flipping mobile homes, mobile home parks, mobile home notes, lease-to-own mobile homes, and mobile home flipping partnerships.

A. Rental Mobile Homes

Rental mobile homes can be an excellent investment option for investors who are looking for a passive income stream. To ensure success with rental mobile homes, investors should consider the following:

Location: The location of the mobile home is a critical factor in attracting tenants. Investors should consider areas where affordable housing is in demand, such as near universities, military bases, or in areas with a growing job market.

Condition of the mobile home: The condition of the mobile home is essential to attracting and retaining tenants. Investors should ensure that the mobile home is in good condition and maintained regularly to ensure that it stays attractive and habitable.

Tenant screening: Screening tenants is an essential part of the rental process to ensure that investors select reliable tenants who can pay rent on time and maintain the mobile home.

Property management: Investors should consider whether they will manage the property themselves or hire a property management company to take care of day-to-day tasks like rent collection, maintenance, and tenant communication.

B. Flipping Mobile Homes

Flipping mobile homes can be an excellent investment option for investors who have experience in construction, renovation, or real estate sales. To ensure success with flipping mobile homes, investors should consider the following:

Purchase price: The purchase price of the mobile home is critical to maximizing the profit potential of a flip. Investors should research the local market and purchase a mobile home at a price that offers potential for renovation and resale at a profit.

Renovation budget: The renovation budget is essential to ensure that the mobile home is updated to meet current market demands. Investors should carefully assess the cost of renovation and ensure that they can complete the project within their budget.

Sales strategy: Investors should carefully plan how they will market and sell the mobile home once renovations are complete. They should consider factors such as the timing of the sale, the target buyer demographic, and the asking price.

C. Mobile Home Parks

Investing in mobile home parks can be an excellent option for investors who are looking for a long-term investment strategy that generates steady rental income. To ensure success with mobile home parks, investors should consider the following:

Market research: Investors should research the local market to understand the demand for affordable housing and assess the competitive landscape of existing mobile home parks.

Location: The location of the mobile home park is a critical factor in attracting tenants. Investors should consider areas with easy access to transportation, shopping, and other amenities.

Management: Investors should be prepared to manage the day-to-day operations of the mobile home park, including rent collection, maintenance, and tenant communication. Investors should consider whether they will manage the park themselves or hire a property management company to take care of these tasks.

D. Mobile Home Notes

Mobile home notes can be an excellent option for investors who are looking for a passive income stream with minimal management requirements. To ensure success with mobile home notes, investors should consider the following:

Creditworthiness of the borrower: The creditworthiness of the borrower is critical to ensuring that the investor will receive timely payments on the loan.

Collateral: The mobile home itself is the collateral for the loan, so investors should ensure that the mobile home is in good condition and that the value of the property covers the loan amount.

Legal documentation: Investors should have a clear and legally binding note agreement that outlines the terms of the loan, including interest rate, payment schedule, and penalties for late payments.

E. Lease-to-Own Mobile Homes

Lease-to-own mobile homes can be an attractive option for tenants who may not have the resources to purchase a mobile home outright. To ensure success with lease-to-own mobile homes, investors should consider the following:

Fair market value: Investors should ensure that the purchase price of the mobile home reflects the fair market value of the property.

Equity build-up: Investors should carefully structure the lease-to-own agreement to ensure that the tenant is gradually building equity in the mobile home over time.

Tenant screening: As with rental mobile homes, screening tenants is an essential part of the lease-to-own process to ensure that investors select reliable tenants who can pay rent on time and maintain the mobile home.

Legal documentation: Investors should have a clear and legally binding lease-to-own agreement that outlines the terms of the lease, including monthly rent payments, equity build-up, and the purchase price of the mobile home.

F. Mobile Home Flipping Partnerships

Mobile home flipping partnerships can be an excellent option for investors who want to share the financial burden and expertise of flipping mobile homes. To ensure success with mobile home flipping partnerships, investors should consider the following:

Partner selection: Investors should carefully select partners who have complementary skills and expertise to contribute to the partnership. It's also essential to establish clear expectations and roles for each partner in the partnership.

Budget and financing: Investors should establish a clear budget and financing plan for the flipping project to ensure that the project stays within budget and that all parties are clear on the financial obligations of the partnership.

Legal documentation: Investors should have a clear and legally binding partnership agreement that outlines the terms of the partnership, including the division of profits and responsibilities.

By exploring the different types of mobile home investments, investors can find the investment strategy that works best for their goals and resources. Regardless of the investment type, it's essential to carefully research the local market, understand the investment's risks and rewards, and establish a solid investment plan to achieve long-term success.

IV. Finding and Evaluating Mobile Homes

Mobile home investors need to have a solid understanding of how to find and evaluate potential investment properties. In this chapter, we'll explore different strategies for finding mobile homes, as well as the key factors to consider when evaluating and inspecting properties.

A. Finding Properties

Real estate agents: Real estate agents can provide access to the Multiple Listing Service (MLS) and offer guidance on pricing and market conditions.

Online listings: Websites such as Zillow, Trulia, and Craigslist, offer a wealth of information on mobile homes for sale. Investors can filter listings by location, price, and other criteria to find properties that meet their investment goals.

Mobile home parks: Mobile home parks can offer a source of potential investment properties. Investors can approach park owners or residents who may be interested in selling their mobile homes.

Auctions: Mobile homes can be purchased at auctions, including government auctions, foreclosure auctions, and online auctions.

Wholesalers: Real estate wholesalers can be a valuable resource for investors looking to find mobile homes for sale. These individuals or companies locate distressed or undervalued properties and sell them at a discount to real estate investors.

Networking: Investors can find potential mobile home investment properties through networking. This can include attending local real estate investor meetings, connecting with local mobile home park owners or managers, or reaching out to other real estate professionals in the area.

B. Evaluating Properties

Location: The location of the mobile home is a critical factor in determining its potential value and rental income. Investors should evaluate the property's proximity to transportation, schools, shopping, and other amenities.

Condition: The condition of the mobile home is another key factor to consider. Investors should evaluate the age of the mobile home, its overall condition, and any needed repairs or renovations.

Rental potential: For rental mobile homes, investors should consider the potential rental income that can be generated by the property. Investors should research the local rental market to understand the demand for affordable housing in the area.

Flipping potential: For flipping mobile homes, investors should consider the potential profit that can be generated by the property. Investors should evaluate the purchase price, renovation costs, and potential sale price of the property to determine whether it can be flipped for a profit.

Zoning laws: Investors should evaluate the zoning laws and regulations in the area where the mobile home is located to ensure that the property can be used for its intended purpose. For example, some areas may have restrictions on the number of mobile homes that can be located on a single property.

Property taxes: Investors should evaluate the property tax rate in the area where the mobile home is located to ensure that it is reasonable and will not impact the investment's profitability.

Maintenance costs: Investors should consider the potential maintenance costs of the mobile home over time, such as repairs, upkeep, and regular maintenance. These costs can impact the profitability of the investment, particularly for rental properties.

Financing options: Investors should evaluate the available financing options for the investment property, such as traditional mortgages, seller financing, or private loans. Understanding the financing options can impact the purchase price and potential profitability of the investment.

C. Inspecting Mobile Homes

Structural integrity: Investors should inspect the mobile home's foundation, framing, and roof to ensure that the structure is sound.

Electrical and plumbing systems: Investors should evaluate the condition of the mobile home's electrical and plumbing systems to ensure that they are functioning correctly.

Heating and cooling systems: Investors should evaluate the mobile home's heating and cooling systems to ensure that they are in good condition and functioning correctly.

Interior condition: Investors should inspect the interior of the mobile home, including walls, floors, and ceilings, to ensure that they are in good condition and free from any significant defects.

Pest control: Investors should inspect the mobile home for signs of pest infestation, such as termites or rodents, which can cause significant damage to the property.

Foundation: The mobile home's foundation is a critical component of its structural integrity. Investors should inspect the foundation for any signs of damage, such as cracks or settling.

Appliances and fixtures: Investors should inspect the mobile home's appliances and fixtures, such as the stove, refrigerator, and air conditioning unit, to ensure that they are in good working condition.

Exterior condition: Investors should inspect the exterior of the mobile home, including the siding, roof, and windows, to ensure that they are in good condition and free from any significant defects.

D. Due Diligence

Title search: Investors should conduct a title search to ensure that the seller has clear title to the mobile home and that there are no liens or encumbrances that could impact the investment.

Homeowner association (HOA) fees: For properties located in mobile home parks, investors should evaluate the HOA fees and any other associated costs to ensure that they are reasonable and will not impact the investment's profitability.

Insurance: Investors should evaluate the cost of insurance for the mobile home to ensure that it is reasonable and will not impact the investment's profitability.

Environmental hazards: Investors should evaluate the mobile home's location for potential environmental hazards, such as flood zones, toxic waste sites, or other hazards that could impact the investment's value.

Legal issues: Investors should conduct a thorough review of any legal issues related to the mobile home, such as zoning violations, building code violations, or other issues that could impact the property's value or use.

Rent history: For rental mobile homes, investors should evaluate the rental history of the property to understand the demand for the property and the potential rental income that can be generated.

Market analysis: Investors should conduct a thorough market analysis of the local real estate market, including the demand for mobile homes, the competition, and the potential for appreciation.

Exit strategy: Investors should have a clear exit strategy in place for the mobile home investment, whether it's a long-term rental or a short-term flip. Understanding the exit strategy can impact the investment's overall profitability.

By taking the time to find and evaluate potential mobile home investment properties, investors can reduce their risks and increase their chances of success. A thorough inspection and due diligence process can help identify any potential issues that could impact the investment's profitability and ensure that the investment meets the investor's goals and resources.

4

FINANCING THE PURCHASE

Financing is an essential component of mobile home investing, and the availability of financing options and the terms of those options can significantly impact an investor's success. In this chapter, we'll explore different financing options available for mobile home investments, as well as creative financing strategies that investors can use to reduce their risks and increase their potential for success.

A. Financing Options

Traditional Mortgages: Investors can finance mobile home investments through traditional mortgages, similar to financing a single-family home. Traditional mortgages require the mobile home to be titled as real estate, and the land on which the mobile home sits is also typically included in the mortgage. The requirements for traditional mortgages can vary, so investors should research different lenders to determine which option is best for their situation.

Personal Loans: Investors can obtain personal loans to finance mobile home investments. Personal loans typically have higher interest rates than traditional mortgages, but they can be a good option for those with less-than-perfect credit. Personal loans can be secured or unsecured and may require collateral.

Private Money: Private money lenders can provide financing for mobile home investments, often with more flexible terms and lower requirements than traditional lenders. Private money lenders can be found through personal networks, online lending platforms, or specialized real estate investment groups. Investors should carefully evaluate the terms of private money loans, as they may have higher interest rates and more stringent repayment terms than other financing options.

Seller Financing: Some sellers may be willing to offer financing for their mobile homes, allowing investors to purchase the property directly from the seller and make payments over time. Seller financing can provide a less formalized and often more flexible option than traditional lending. However, investors should evaluate the terms of seller financing carefully, as the interest rates and repayment terms may be less favorable than other financing options.

Partnership or Joint Venture: Investors can partner with others to pool resources and invest in mobile homes together. This can provide more resources and increase the potential for profit. Joint venture agreements can be formalized through legal contracts and should specify each party's roles, responsibilities, and share of profits. However, investors should carefully evaluate potential partners and ensure that their goals and expectations align before entering into a partnership.

Equity Lines of Credit: Investors can use equity lines of credit on other properties they own to finance mobile home investments. This strategy can be advantageous for investors with significant equity in other properties and can provide a flexible source of financing. However, investors should carefully evaluate the risks and benefits of using equity lines of credit, as they may have higher interest rates and more stringent repayment terms than other financing options.

FHA Loans: The Federal Housing Administration (FHA) offers loans for mobile homes, including Title I loans for home improvements and Title II loans for the purchase of mobile homes and land. FHA loans typically have lower down payment requirements and more flexible credit score requirements than traditional mortgages. However, FHA loans may have higher interest rates and require mortgage insurance premiums, which can increase the overall cost of the loan.

B. Credit Scores and Financing

Credit scores are a critical factor in obtaining financing for mobile home investments, and lenders evaluate credit scores to assess an individual's creditworthiness and ability to repay a loan. Investors should take steps to improve their credit scores before applying for financing, including paying bills on time, reducing debt, and disputing any errors on their credit report. Additionally, investors should understand the factors that impact their credit scores:

Credit Score Range: Credit scores range from 300 to 850, with higher scores indicating better creditworthiness. The credit score range can impact the availability of financing options and the interest rates offered by lenders.

Credit Utilization: Credit utilization, or the amount of credit used compared to the total available credit, is an important factor in credit scores. Investors should aim to keep their credit utilization below 30% to maintain good credit scores. High credit utilization can signal to lenders that an individual is overextended and may have difficulty repaying debt.

Length of Credit History: The length of an individual's credit history is another important factor in credit scores. Investors should establish credit early and maintain good credit habits over time to build a strong credit history. A long credit history can demonstrate to lenders an individual's ability to manage credit responsibly.

C. Loan Application Process

The loan application process for mobile home financing is similar to the process for traditional home financing. Investors will need to provide personal and financial information, as well as information on the mobile home they wish to purchase. Lenders will evaluate the application and assess the risk of the investment, including the borrower's creditworthiness and the value of the mobile home. The loan application process typically includes the following steps:

Pre-Approval: Investors should consider obtaining pre-approval for financing before making an offer on a mobile home investment. Pre-approval can provide the investor with a clear understanding of their financing options and increase the likelihood of their offer being accepted.

Application: Once an investor identifies a mobile home they wish to purchase, they will need to complete a loan application with a lender. The application will require personal and financial information, as well as information on the mobile home.

Underwriting: After submitting the loan application, the lender will evaluate the application and assess the risk of the investment. The lender will evaluate the borrower's creditworthiness, the value of the mobile home, and other factors to determine whether to approve the loan.

Closing: Once the loan is approved, the investor will need to sign the loan documents and pay any closing costs associated with the purchase. Closing costs can include appraisal fees, title search fees, and other expenses.

D. Creative Financing Strategies

Lease Option: Investors can use a lease option to acquire mobile homes with little or no money down. With a lease option, the investor leases the mobile home from the seller with the option to purchase the property at a later date. This option can be advantageous for investors with limited resources or those who want to test a property before committing to a purchase.

Owner Financing: Investors can use owner financing to purchase mobile homes directly from the seller. The seller acts as the lender, providing financing for the purchase. This option can be advantageous for investors who do not meet traditional lending requirements or who want to negotiate more flexible terms with the seller.

Private Money Lending: Private money lenders can provide financing for mobile home investments with more flexible terms and lower requirements than traditional lenders. Private money lenders can be found through personal networks, online lending platforms, or specialized real estate investment groups. Investors should carefully evaluate the terms of private money loans, as they may have higher interest rates and more stringent repayment terms than other financing options.

Hard Money Lending: Hard money lenders can provide short-term financing for mobile home investments, often with higher interest rates than traditional lenders. Hard money loans are typically secured by the mobile home and provide quick access to funds.

Crowdfunding: Crowdfunding platforms can provide financing for mobile home investments through collective investments. Investors can pool their resources with other investors to purchase mobile homes together. Crowdfunding can provide access to larger investment opportunities and can spread risks among multiple investors.

Subject-to Financing: Investors can purchase mobile homes subject-to the existing financing on the property, which can be advantageous in situations where the existing financing has favorable terms. With subject-to financing, the investor takes over the existing mortgage payments and assumes ownership of the property but does not assume liability for the mortgage. This option can be advantageous for investors with limited resources or those who want to acquire properties quickly.

By understanding the different financing options available and utilizing creative financing strategies, investors can reduce their risks and increase their potential for success. Improving credit scores, understanding the loan application process, and utilizing pre-approval can all increase the likelihood of obtaining financing for mobile home investments.

Investors should evaluate the various financing options available and determine which option best suits their investment goals and resources. Creative financing strategies can provide alternative financing solutions, but investors should carefully evaluate the risks and benefits of each strategy before moving forward.

In the next chapter, we'll explore the process of managing and maintaining mobile home investments, including managing rental properties and preparing for the unexpected.

5

MANAGING YOUR INVESTMENTS

Mobile home management is a critical component of mobile home investing, requiring attention to detail and a commitment to providing safe, comfortable housing for tenants. Effective mobile home management involves a range of activities, including finding and screening tenants, creating lease agreements, maintaining the property, and mitigating risks.

A. Finding Tenants

Finding tenants for mobile homes can be a challenging process, particularly in areas with high vacancy rates. Investors can use a variety of marketing strategies to find potential tenants, including online listings, classified ads, and word of mouth. Social media platforms can also be an effective way to market mobile homes, particularly to younger tenants.

To attract potential tenants, investors should create detailed listings that include photographs and detailed descriptions of the mobile home and amenities. Listings should be clear and concise, highlighting the features and benefits of the property. Investors can also offer incentives, such as move-in specials or free rent for the first month, to attract potential tenants.

B. Screening Tenants

Screening tenants is a critical step in the mobile home management process. Investors should conduct thorough background and credit checks to assess the tenant's ability to pay rent and maintain the property. Screening should include the following steps:

1. Application: Tenants should complete a rental application that includes personal and financial information, employment history, and rental history.

2. Background Check: Investors should conduct a background check to assess the tenant's criminal history and verify their identity.

3. Credit Check: Investors should also conduct a credit check to assess the tenant's creditworthiness and ability to pay rent.

4. References: Investors should contact the tenant's previous landlords and personal references to assess their reliability and ability to maintain the property.

C. Lease Agreements

Creating a comprehensive lease agreement is essential to protect the investor's interests and ensure a clear understanding between the tenant and landlord. Lease agreements should include the following information:

1. Rent Amount: The lease agreement should clearly state the monthly rent amount and any fees or deposits required.

2. Term: The lease agreement should clearly state the length of the lease and the conditions for renewal.

3. Tenant Responsibilities: The lease agreement should clearly outline the tenant's responsibilities, including maintaining

the property, paying utilities, and reporting any damages or necessary repairs.

4. Landlord Responsibilities: The lease agreement should also outline the landlord's responsibilities, including maintaining the property and addressing any necessary repairs.

5. Late Fees: The lease agreement should include a late fee policy for late rent payments.

6. Termination Policy: The lease agreement should include a termination policy, outlining the conditions for terminating the lease.

D. Maintenance and Repairs

Maintaining mobile homes is essential to ensure the property remains safe and comfortable for tenants. Investors should establish a regular maintenance schedule to address routine repairs and maintenance tasks, such as lawn care and pest control. Repairs should be addressed promptly to minimize tenant inconvenience and prevent further damage to the property.

Investors should also establish a plan for emergency repairs and make sure tenants have a way to report urgent maintenance issues. It's essential to maintain a good relationship with tenants, address their concerns promptly, and keep the property in good condition to minimize vacancies and maintain a steady stream of rental income.

E. Landlord-Tenant Laws

Understanding landlord-tenant laws is critical to ensuring compliance and avoiding legal issues. Investors should be aware of state and local laws governing mobile home rentals and ensure they comply with these laws. Landlord-tenant laws cover areas such as security deposits, evictions, and rental agreements, and vary from state to state.

F. Property Insurance

Investors should carry property insurance to protect their investment from damages or liability issues. Insurance policies should be reviewed regularly to ensure adequate coverage and compliance with local laws. Investors should consult with insurance agents familiar with mobile home investments to ensure they have the right coverage for their property.

G. Professional Assistance

Mobile home management can be a complex and time-consuming process, requiring a range of skills and knowledge. Investors can benefit from the assistance of professionals, including attorneys, property managers, and contractors with experience in mobile home investing. These professionals can provide valuable insights and assistance in the mobile home investing process, from finding and evaluating properties to managing and maintaining them.

H. Tenant Retention

Retaining tenants is essential for maintaining a steady stream of rental income and avoiding the costs associated with vacancy. Investors can improve tenant retention by addressing maintenance and repair issues promptly, providing a positive tenant experience, and being responsive to tenant needs.

Effective communication with tenants is also critical. Investors should establish a clear and open line of communication with tenants to address any concerns or issues promptly. This can include providing multiple ways for tenants to contact the landlord, such as email, phone, or text messaging.

I. Risk Management

Mobile home investing is not without risks, and investors should take steps to manage these risks effectively. Strategies for risk management can include carrying adequate insurance coverage, screening tenants thoroughly, and maintaining the property regularly to prevent potential hazards.

Investors should also establish a contingency plan for unexpected events, such as natural disasters or tenant emergencies. A contingency plan should include a clear course of action for addressing emergencies, such as evacuating the property or providing temporary housing for displaced tenants.

By implementing effective mobile home management strategies and staying up-to-date with industry trends and best practices, investors can maximize returns and minimize risks. Effective mobile home management requires attention to detail, a commitment to maintaining the property, and a willingness to invest in the resources necessary to provide a safe, comfortable living environment for tenants.

In the next chapter, we'll explore how investors can prepare for the unexpected and navigate potential challenges in the mobile home investing process.

6

LEGAL CONSIDERATIONS

Investing in mobile homes involves navigating a complex legal framework of federal, state, and local regulations. From zoning and building codes to licensing and permits, tenant-landlord laws, and financing and lending practices, mobile home investors must comply with a range of regulations to avoid legal issues and financial penalties.

A. Local Regulations

Local regulations play a critical role in mobile home investing. They govern many aspects of the investment process, including zoning and building codes, permitting, licensing, and tenant-landlord laws. These regulations can vary widely depending on the location, so investors should thoroughly research local regulations before investing in mobile homes to ensure they comply with all legal requirements.

For example, some localities may prohibit the operation of mobile home parks in certain areas, while others may have strict requirements for the installation of mobile homes. Investors should seek legal counsel or other professional advice to ensure they understand the rules and regulations in their area.

B. State Regulations

State regulations also impact mobile home investing. These regulations cover a range of issues, including property taxes, titling, sales taxes, and licensing requirements. Investors must understand state regulations and requirements when investing in mobile homes, as they can have a significant impact on the financial viability of the investment.

For instance, some states require a license to operate a mobile home park, while others have strict regulations governing the titling and transfer of mobile homes. Understanding state regulations and requirements is critical to the success of a mobile home investment.

C. Federal Regulations

Federal regulations also play a role in mobile home investing. The Department of Housing and Urban Development (HUD) sets standards for the design and construction of mobile homes, while the Consumer Financial Protection Bureau (CFPB) regulates financing and lending practices for mobile home investments.

Investors should be aware of federal regulations that impact mobile home investing and take steps to comply with these regulations. For example, HUD regulations require that all manufactured homes meet specific design and construction standards, while the CFPB regulates lending practices, including disclosures, fees, and interest rates.

D. Legal Documents

Investors must prepare and maintain a range of legal documents related to mobile home investments, including purchase agreements, lease agreements, and other contracts. These documents should be drafted carefully to ensure they comply with all legal requirements and protect the investor's interests.

For example, lease agreements should clearly outline the terms of the tenancy, including rent, security deposits, and the responsibilities of the landlord and tenant. Purchase agreements should specify the purchase price, financing terms, and any contingencies related to the sale.

Investors should consult with legal professionals to ensure they understand the legal requirements for these documents and have the necessary protection in place.

E. Evictions

Evictions can be a time-consuming and costly process for mobile home investors. Investors must understand the eviction process and the legal requirements for eviction in their area.

Clear communication with tenants, addressing concerns promptly, and providing a positive tenant experience can all help reduce the likelihood of eviction. Investors should also seek legal counsel if they must go through an eviction to ensure they follow all legal requirements.

F. Taxes

Mobile home investments are subject to a variety of taxes, including property taxes, sales taxes, and income taxes. Investors should understand the tax implications of their mobile home investments and take steps to minimize tax liability.

Working with a qualified tax professional can provide investors with valuable insights and guidance on tax planning and compliance. Investors should ensure they are aware of all tax requirements in their area and maintain accurate financial records to facilitate compliance with tax regulations.

G. Insurance

Investors must carry adequate insurance coverage for their mobile home investments. Insurance can protect against property damage, liability claims, and other risks associated with mobile home investments.

Investors should consult with an insurance professional to ensure they have the necessary insurance coverage for their investment. Coverage options may include property and casualty insurance, liability insurance, and specialized insurance for mobile home parks.

Mobile home park owners may also need to carry workers' compensation insurance and other types of coverage to comply with local and state regulations.

By understanding the legal considerations of mobile home investing, investors can minimize risks, avoid legal issues and financial penalties, and protect their investments. It's essential to maintain accurate and complete records, work with legal and tax professionals, and comply with all federal, state, and local regulations to ensure a successful mobile home investment.

Investors should also stay informed of changes in laws and regulations that may impact their mobile home investments. These changes can include new zoning or building codes, changes in tenant-landlord laws, or changes to financing and lending practices.

It's also important to work with trusted professionals, including attorneys, tax advisors, insurance professionals, and real estate agents with experience in mobile home investments. These professionals can provide valuable guidance and support throughout the investment process.

In the next chapter, we'll explore the importance of ongoing education and networking for mobile home investors. By continuing to learn and connect with others in the industry, investors can stay up-to-date on trends and best practices and increase their chances of success in the mobile home market.

7

Risks and Rewards

Mobile home investing, like any investment, involves both risks and rewards. Investors must carefully evaluate the risks and rewards to make informed decisions about their investments. In this chapter, we'll explore the risks and rewards of mobile home investing and strategies for balancing these factors.

A. Risks of Mobile Home Investing

Mobile home investing comes with certain risks that investors should be aware of. Some of the common risks of mobile home investing include:

Lack of appreciation: Mobile homes may not appreciate in value as much as other types of real estate investments. This can limit the potential for long-term gains.

Limited financing options: Financing options for mobile home investments may be more limited than for other types of real estate investments. This can make it more difficult to secure financing for investments.

Maintenance and repair costs: Mobile homes may require more frequent maintenance and repairs than other types of real estate investments. This can add to the overall cost of the investment and reduce potential profits.

Tenant turnover: Mobile homes typically have higher tenant turnover rates than other types of rental properties. This can lead to more frequent vacancies and higher costs associated with finding new tenants.

Local regulations: Local and state regulations can impact the profitability of mobile home investments. This can include zoning restrictions, rent control laws, and other regulations that can limit the potential for profits.

B. Rewards of Mobile Home Investing

Mobile home investing also offers unique rewards that investors should consider when evaluating potential investments. Some of the benefits of mobile home investing include:

Affordability: Mobile homes are often more affordable than other types of real estate investments, making it easier to enter the market. This can provide a lower barrier to entry for new investors.

Cash flow: Mobile home investments can provide stable cash flow from rental income. This can provide a reliable source of income for investors.

Lower barriers to entry: Mobile home investing may have lower barriers to entry than other types of real estate investments, allowing more investors to enter the market. This can provide more opportunities for investors to participate in the market.

Market demand: The demand for affordable housing continues to grow, making mobile home investments a potentially lucrative market. This can provide a strong potential for profit in the long-term.

C. Balancing Risks and Rewards

Balancing the risks and rewards of mobile home investing is essential to making informed investment decisions. Investors should evaluate potential investments based on their investment goals, risk tolerance, and available resources.

To balance the risks and rewards of mobile home investing, investors should consider:

Due diligence: Conduct thorough due diligence on potential investments to assess the risks and potential rewards. This can include researching the market, evaluating the property, and reviewing the financials.

Diversification: Diversify investments across multiple properties or markets to minimize risk. This can provide a buffer against potential losses and help to spread risk.

Ongoing education: Continuously educate oneself on the latest trends and best practices in mobile home investing. This can provide valuable insights and help to inform investment decisions.

Networking: Connect with other mobile home investors and professionals to gain valuable insights and support. This can provide access to resources and help to inform investment decisions.

Market conditions: Stay informed about market conditions and adjust investment strategies accordingly to maximize returns and minimize risks. This can include keeping an eye on economic indicators, evaluating supply and demand in the market, and monitoring market trends.

Exit strategies: Develop a plan for selling the property or transferring ownership in the future to maximize returns and minimize potential losses. This can include evaluating potential resale values, considering tax implications, and developing a plan for transferring ownership.

By balancing the risks and rewards of mobile home investing, investors can make informed investment decisions and increase their chances of success in the market.

8

SCALING UP TO REWARD YOURSELF MORE

Mobile home investing can be a profitable business, but to grow your portfolio and increase your income, you need to scale up your operations. In this chapter, we'll explore some strategies for scaling up your mobile home investing business.

A. Growing Your Portfolio

One of the best ways to scale up your mobile home investing business is to grow your portfolio. This means buying more mobile homes and expanding your investment portfolio. Here are some tips for growing your portfolio:

1. Set clear investment goals: Before expanding your portfolio, define your investment goals. This will help you identify the type of properties you want to invest in, the return on investment you're looking for, and the time frame you want to achieve your goals.

2. Identify profitable markets: Research and identify markets that offer good returns on investment. Look for areas with high demand for affordable housing, growing populations, and low vacancy rates.

3. Create a system for managing properties: As your portfolio

grows, managing properties can become time-consuming. Create a system for managing properties, including tenant screening, rent collection, and maintenance.

4. Leverage other investors: Consider partnering with other investors to pool resources and share the risks and rewards of investing in mobile homes.

B. Hiring Property Managers

As your portfolio grows, you may need to hire property managers to help manage your properties. Property managers can help you:

1. Handle day-to-day operations: Property managers can handle the day-to-day operations of managing properties, including rent collection, tenant screening, and maintenance.

2. Maximize rental income: Property managers can help you set appropriate rental rates to maximize your rental income.

3. Save time: Hiring property managers can free up your time, allowing you to focus on expanding your portfolio and growing your business.

4. Ensure compliance with local regulations: Property managers can help ensure compliance with local regulations, reducing the risk of legal issues and fines.

C. Outsourcing Maintenance and Repairs

Outsourcing maintenance and repairs can be an effective way to scale up your mobile home investing business. Here are some benefits of outsourcing maintenance and repairs:

1. Save time and money: Outsourcing maintenance and repairs can save you time and money. You won't have to spend time

on repairs, and you can avoid the cost of purchasing tools and equipment.

2. Access to professional services: By outsourcing maintenance and repairs, you can access professional services from contractors who specialize in mobile home repairs.

3. Improve tenant satisfaction: Outsourcing maintenance and repairs can improve tenant satisfaction, as repairs are completed quickly and professionally.

4. Reduce liability: Outsourcing maintenance and repairs can help reduce liability, as professional contractors are often licensed, insured, and trained to handle repairs safely and efficiently.

Scaling up your mobile home investing business requires careful planning and execution. By growing your portfolio, hiring property managers, and outsourcing maintenance and repairs, you can increase your income, reduce your workload, and achieve your investment goals.

X. Marketing Your Mobile Home Investments

Mobile home investing can be a lucrative business, but to maximize returns, investors must develop effective marketing strategies. In this chapter, we'll explore key elements of marketing mobile home investments, including creating a marketing plan, advertising properties, building a brand, and connecting with other investors through real estate investor associations.

A. Creating a Marketing Plan

A marketing plan is a blueprint for reaching target customers and achieving investment goals. To create a marketing plan for mobile home investments, investors should consider the following:

Identify the target audience: Investors should identify the target audience for their mobile home investments. This includes determining the demographics and psychographics of potential tenants or buyers.

Establish investment goals: Investors should establish clear investment goals, including the desired return on investment, cash flow, and time frame.

Develop a unique selling proposition: Investors should develop a unique selling proposition for their mobile home investments. This includes identifying what sets their properties apart from the competition, such as affordable pricing, attractive amenities, or convenient location.

Choose marketing channels: Investors should choose the most effective marketing channels for their mobile home investments. This includes online listings, classified ads, social media, and word of mouth.

B. Advertising Your Properties

Advertising is a critical component of marketing mobile home investments. Effective advertising can help attract potential tenants or buyers and generate leads. Some key strategies for advertising mobile home investments include:

Online listings: Investors should list their mobile homes on popular online real estate marketplaces, such as Zillow, Redfin, or Realtor.co m.

Classified ads: Investors can advertise their mobile homes in classified ads in local newspapers or online classified sites, such as Craigslist.

Social media: Investors can use social media platforms, such as Facebook, Instagram, and Twitter, to advertise their mobile homes to potential tenants or buyers.

Direct mail: Investors can use direct mail campaigns to reach potential buyers or tenants through targeted marketing.

C. Building a Brand

Building a brand is essential to establishing a successful mobile home investing business. A strong brand can help investors differentiate their properties from the competition and build trust with potential tenants or buyers. Some key strategies for building a brand in mobile home investing include:

Creating a logo and brand identity: Investors should develop a unique logo and brand identity that reflects the unique selling proposition of their mobile home investments.

Creating a website: Investors should create a professional website for their mobile home investments that showcases their properties, provides information about the investment, and offers an easy way for potential tenants or buyers to contact them.

Providing excellent customer service: Investors should prioritize providing excellent customer service to tenants or buyers, which can help build a positive reputation for their brand and attract new business.

D. Connecting with Other Investors through Real Estate Investor Associations

Real estate investor associations (REIAs) provide valuable opportunities for networking and learning about the latest trends and best practices in mobile home investing. Some key benefits of joining a REIA include:

Networking opportunities: REIAs provide opportunities to connect with other mobile home investors, share experiences and knowledge, and establish valuable partnerships.

Education and training: REIAs offer educational resources and training programs to help investors stay informed about the latest trends and best practices in mobile home investing.

Access to resources: REIAs provide access to a range of resources, including legal and financial advice, marketing resources, and investment tools.

By focusing on creating a marketing plan, advertising properties, building a brand, and connecting with other investors through real estate investor associations, mobile home investors can increase their chances of success in the market.

9

WHAT TO DO WHEN IT'S TIME TO CASH OUT

Exit strategies are an important part of mobile home investing. Whether an investor is looking to liquidate a mobile home park or sell a rental property, it's essential to have a plan in place to maximize returns and minimize potential losses. In this chapter, we'll explore common exit strategies for mobile home investing.

A. Selling Mobile Homes

Selling mobile homes is a common exit strategy for mobile home investors. There are several ways to sell mobile homes, including:

Selling to a homeowner: Mobile homes can be sold directly to a homeowner, similar to traditional real estate.

Selling to a dealer: Investors can sell mobile homes to dealers who will then resell the property.

Selling to a mobile home park: Some mobile home parks may be interested in purchasing additional properties to add to their park.

Selling at auction: Mobile homes can be sold at auction, either online or in-person.

Before selling a mobile home, it's important to conduct a thorough analysis of the property's value and market conditions to determine the best selling strategy.

B. Liquidating Mobile Home Parks

Liquidating a mobile home park is another common exit strategy for mobile home investors. This strategy involves selling off individual mobile homes and/or the land itself. Some investors may choose to sell the mobile home park to another investor, while others may opt to sell to a developer for other purposes.

When liquidating a mobile home park, it's important to consider the potential tax implications and the best selling strategy to maximize returns and minimize losses.

C. Exiting Rental Properties

Exiting rental properties is another common exit strategy for mobile home investors. This strategy can involve selling the property to another investor, converting the property into a different use, or simply ceasing rental operations.

When exiting a rental property, it's important to consider the current market conditions, potential tax implications, and the best strategy for maximizing returns and minimizing potential losses.

In addition to these common exit strategies, investors should also consider the benefits of Real Estate Investor Associations (REIA). These associations can provide valuable resources and networking opportunities for investors, as well as access to the latest industry trends and best practices.

By considering the various exit strategies and utilizing the resources provided by REIAs, investors can make informed decisions about their mobile home investments and maximize their returns in the market.

In the final chapter, we'll provide a summary of the key takeaways from this book and offer some final thoughts on mobile home investing.

10

DON'T FALL INTO THESE COMMON PITFALLS

Mobile home investing can be a lucrative business if done correctly. However, there are common mistakes that investors should avoid in order to maximize their chances of success. In this chapter, we'll explore the common mistakes to avoid in mobile home investing and how to learn from them.

A. Lessons from Failed Investments

One of the best ways to learn how to avoid mistakes is to study past failures. Investors should review their failed investments and take note of what went wrong. Some of the common mistakes that lead to failed mobile home investments include:

Overpaying for properties: Overpaying for a mobile home can result in negative cash flow and reduce the profitability of the investment.

Ignoring maintenance: Neglecting maintenance can lead to costly repairs and cause tenants to leave.

Lack of due diligence: Failing to conduct due diligence can result in hidden surprises, such as zoning issues, code violations, or liens.

Poor tenant screening: Poor tenant screening can result in difficult tenants who cause damage to the property or fail to pay rent.

Failing to adapt: Failing to adapt to changes in the market or tenant needs can result in a decline in demand for the property.

B. How to Prevent Costly Errors

To avoid costly mistakes, mobile home investors should take a proactive approach. Here are some strategies to prevent errors:

Thorough due diligence: Conduct thorough due diligence before purchasing a property to identify any issues that may impact the investment.

Careful financial analysis: Perform a careful financial analysis to ensure that the investment will generate positive cash flow.

Effective tenant screening: Screen potential tenants carefully to ensure that they will be reliable, responsible renters.

Regular maintenance and repairs: Schedule regular maintenance and repairs to prevent small problems from turning into costly repairs.

Adapt to market changes: Stay up-to-date on market trends and tenant needs to ensure that the property remains competitive and in demand.

C. Learning from Mistakes

Even the most experienced mobile home investors can make mistakes. The key is to learn from these mistakes and use them as an opportunity to improve. Here are some strategies for learning from mistakes:

Evaluate failures: After a failed investment, conduct a thorough evaluation to identify the root cause of the problem.

Identify solutions: Once the cause of the problem has been identified, develop a plan to correct it.

Adapt: Implement changes to the investment strategy based on the lessons learned from the failed investment.

Seek advice: Seek advice from experienced investors or professionals to gain insights and identify best practices.

Continued learning: Stay up-to-date on the latest trends and best practices in mobile home investing to improve investment strategies and prevent future mistakes.

By learning from past mistakes and taking a proactive approach to mobile home investing, investors can reduce the risks and increase their chances of success in the market.

In the final chapter, we'll summarize the key takeaways from this book and offer some final thoughts on mobile home investing.

11

FAREWELL

As we come to the end of this book, it's clear that mobile home investing can be a profitable and worthwhile investment strategy. Throughout this book, we've explored the unique advantages and challenges of investing in mobile homes, including the potential for stable cash flow, the lower barriers to entry, and the challenges of financing and managing mobile home properties.

In this final chapter, we'll provide a recap of the key points we've covered in this book, discuss the future outlook for mobile home investing, and offer some final thoughts on the subject.

Throughout this book, we've covered a wide range of topics related to mobile home investing, including:

- The advantages and disadvantages of investing in mobile homes
- The different types of mobile home investments, including parks and individual properties
- Strategies for financing mobile home investments, including traditional mortgages and creative financing options
- Best practices for managing and maintaining mobile home

investments, including finding and screening tenants, lease agreements, and maintenance and repairs

- The legal considerations of mobile home investing, including local, state, and federal regulations and legal documents
- The risks and rewards of mobile home investing and strategies for balancing these factors
- How to scale up your mobile home investing business, including growing your portfolio, hiring property managers, and outsourcing maintenance and repairs
- Strategies for marketing your mobile home investments, including creating a marketing plan, advertising your properties, and building a brand
- Exit strategies for mobile home investments, including selling properties, liquidating mobile home parks, and exiting rental properties
- Common mistakes to avoid when investing in mobile homes

By understanding these key points and incorporating them into your investment strategy, you can increase your chances of success in the mobile home investing market.

The future outlook for mobile home investing is positive, as the demand for affordable housing continues to grow. The affordable housing crisis in the US has created a significant demand for mobile homes, and this trend is expected to continue. The increasing popularity of tiny homes and the growing interest in sustainable living may also drive the demand for mobile home investments.

Mobile home investing is not without its challenges, but it can be a profitable and worthwhile investment strategy. By taking the time to educate yourself on the unique aspects of mobile home investments and utilizing best practices, you can reduce your risks and increase your chances of success in this market. As with any investment, it's important to conduct thorough due diligence and stay informed about market trends and conditions.

We hope that this book has provided you with valuable insights and information on mobile home investing. Whether you're a seasoned real estate investor or just getting started in the industry, we wish you success in your mobile home investing endeavors.

Made in the USA
Monee, IL
04 November 2026

67376106R00036